**MINI MAKERS**

by Megan Borgert-Spaniol

a Capstone company — publishers for children

Raintree is an imprint of Capstone Global Library Limited, a company incorporated in England and Wales having its registered office at 264 Banbury Road, Oxford, OX2 7DY – Registered company number: 6695582

www.raintree.co.uk
myorders@raintree.co.uk

Hardback edition © Capstone Global Library Limited 2024
Paperback edition © Capstone Global Library Limited 2025
The moral rights of the proprietor have been asserted.

All rights reserved. No part of this publication may be reproduced in any form or by any means (including photocopying or storing it in any medium by electronic means and whether or not transiently or incidentally to some other use of this publication) without the written permission of the copyright owner, except in accordance with the provisions of the Copyright, Designs and Patents Act 1988 or under the terms of a licence issued by the Copyright Licensing Agency, 5th Floor, Shackleton House, 4 Battle Bridge Lane, London, SE1 2HX (www.cla.co.uk). Applications for the copyright owner's written permission should be addressed to the publisher.

Edited by: Jessica Rusick
Designed by: Aruna Rangarajan, Sarah DeYoung
Originated by Capstone Global Library Ltd

ISBN 978 1 3982 5168 7 (hardback)
ISBN 978 1 3982 5173 1 (paperback)

**British Library Cataloguing in Publication Data**
A full catalogue record for this book is available from the British Library.

**Acknowledgements**
We would like to thank the following for permission to reproduce photographs: iStockphoto: avean (font), Front Cover, 1, Back Cover; Mighty Media, Inc.: 5 (pencil), project photos; Shutterstock: Casey Elise Christopher (cat), 22, 23, don padungvichean, 17 (trinket), donatas1205, 5 (right), Feng Yu, 5 (left), I-ing, 23 (wipe-clean board), kak2s, Front Cover (key), marcin jucha, Front Cover (push pin), Somchai Som, Front Cover (coins), TabitaZn, Back Cover (gift tag)

Design Elements: iStockphoto: Tolga TEZCAN; Shutterstock: ds_vector, Valerii_M

Every effort has been made to contact copyright holders of material reproduced in this book. Any omissions will be rectified in subsequent printings if notice is given to the publisher.

All the internet addresses (URLs) given in this book were valid at the time of going to press. However, due to the dynamic nature of the internet, some addresses may have changed, or sites may have changed or ceased to exist since publication. While the author and publisher regret any inconvenience this may cause readers, no responsibility for any such changes can be accepted by either the author or the publisher.

Printed and bound in India

# CONTENTS

Mini projects .................................................. 4

Mini bunting .................................................. 6

Mini worry monster ..................................... 8

Mini bulletin board .................................... 10

Mini Zen garden ......................................... 12

Mini drawer fresheners ........................... 14

Mini terrarium ............................................ 16

Mini lamp ..................................................... 18

Mini frame magnets ................................. 20

Mini bag throw .......................................... 24

Mini tapestry .............................................. 28

Find out more ............................................ 32

About the author ...................................... 32

# MINI PROJECTS

What better way to make a space your own than filling it with homemade decorations? The creations in this book are cute, colourful and – best of all – mini! Style your space with these petite projects.

Hang some **teeny-weeny bunting** above your desk for a spot of cheer and colour.

Bring nature indoors with a **tiny terrarium** or **mini Zen garden**.

Or craft a **little lamp** to light up the night.

Whatever you choose, these mini projects will make your space **UNIQUELY YOURS!**

## BASIC SUPPLIES

- » coloured card
- » cardboard
- » craft sticks
- » felt
- » hot-glue gun
- » felt-tip pens
- » paint and paintbrushes
- » patterned paper
- » ruler
- » scissors
- » string
- » tape

# Crafting tips

**SET YOURSELF UP FOR SUCCESS!** Read through the materials and instructions before starting a project. Cover your workspace with paper or plastic to protect it from messes or spills.

**LET YOUR CREATIVITY SHINE!** Put your own stamp on these projects. Don't be afraid to make changes or try something new!

**UPCYCLE!** Lots of the projects in this book use materials you'll probably find around your home. Is there something you can't find? Think of ways to adapt the project using items you do have.

**ASK FIRST!** Get permission to do the projects and to use any materials you find at home or school.

**SAFETY FIRST!** Ask an adult for help with projects that require sharp or hot tools.

**CLEAN UP!** When you've finished crafting, make sure you put away any supplies you took out. Clean up any spills and wipe down your crafting surface.

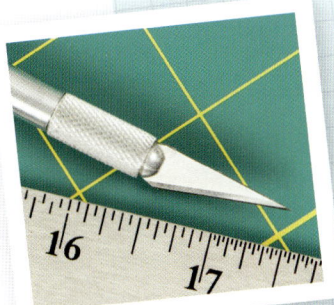

# Mini BUNTING

Raise this mini bunting above your desk, a plant or even a birthday cake!

## MATERIALS

- » cardboard
- » scissors
- » ruler
- » fabric scraps
- » marker pen
- » string
- » hot-glue gun
- » wooden skewers
- » items to hold skewers upright

**1**

Cut out a cardboard triangle with sides no longer than 2.5 centimetres.

**2**

Trace the cardboard triangle on scraps of fabric to create 12 to 16 flags.

**3**

Cut out the triangle flags.

**4**

Cut a piece of string about 40 centimetres long. Glue the flags along the string.

## 5

Tie each end of the string to a wooden skewer. Cut off any excess string.

## 6

Stick the wooden skewers in anything that will hold them upright, such as clay, floral oasis, a potted plant or a delicious dessert!

# Mini WORRY MONSTER

Worry monsters help children to work through what's bothering them. Whisper your worries to this friendly creature and see how it makes you feel!

**MATERIALS**
- » lid about 8cm across
- » felt
- » felt-tip pen
- » scissors
- » hot-glue gun
- » cotton-wool balls
- » pom-poms
- » googly eyes
- » white beads

## 1

Trace the lid on the felt twice to create two circles. Cut out the circles.

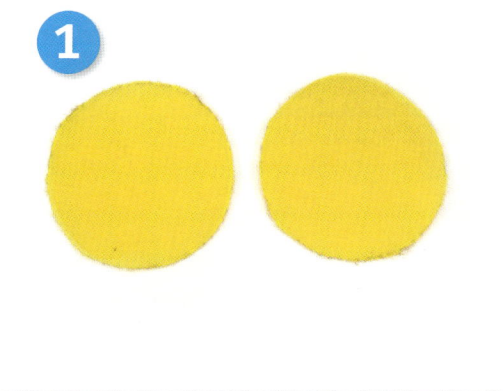

## 2

Spread hot glue around the edge of one circle, leaving about 2.5 cm of the edge unglued.

## 3

Lay the second circle on top of the first so their edges stick together.

## 4

Fold the circular pouch inside out. Stuff it with cotton wool balls.

## 5

Fold in the edges of the unglued pouch section and glue them together to create a clean seam. This is the monster's body.

## 6

Glue pom-poms onto the body to create hands and feet. Glue googly eyes to the monster's face.

## 7

Cut out a felt mouth and glue it below the monster's eyes. Glue white beads onto the mouth for teeth. Talk to your little monster whenever you have a worry!

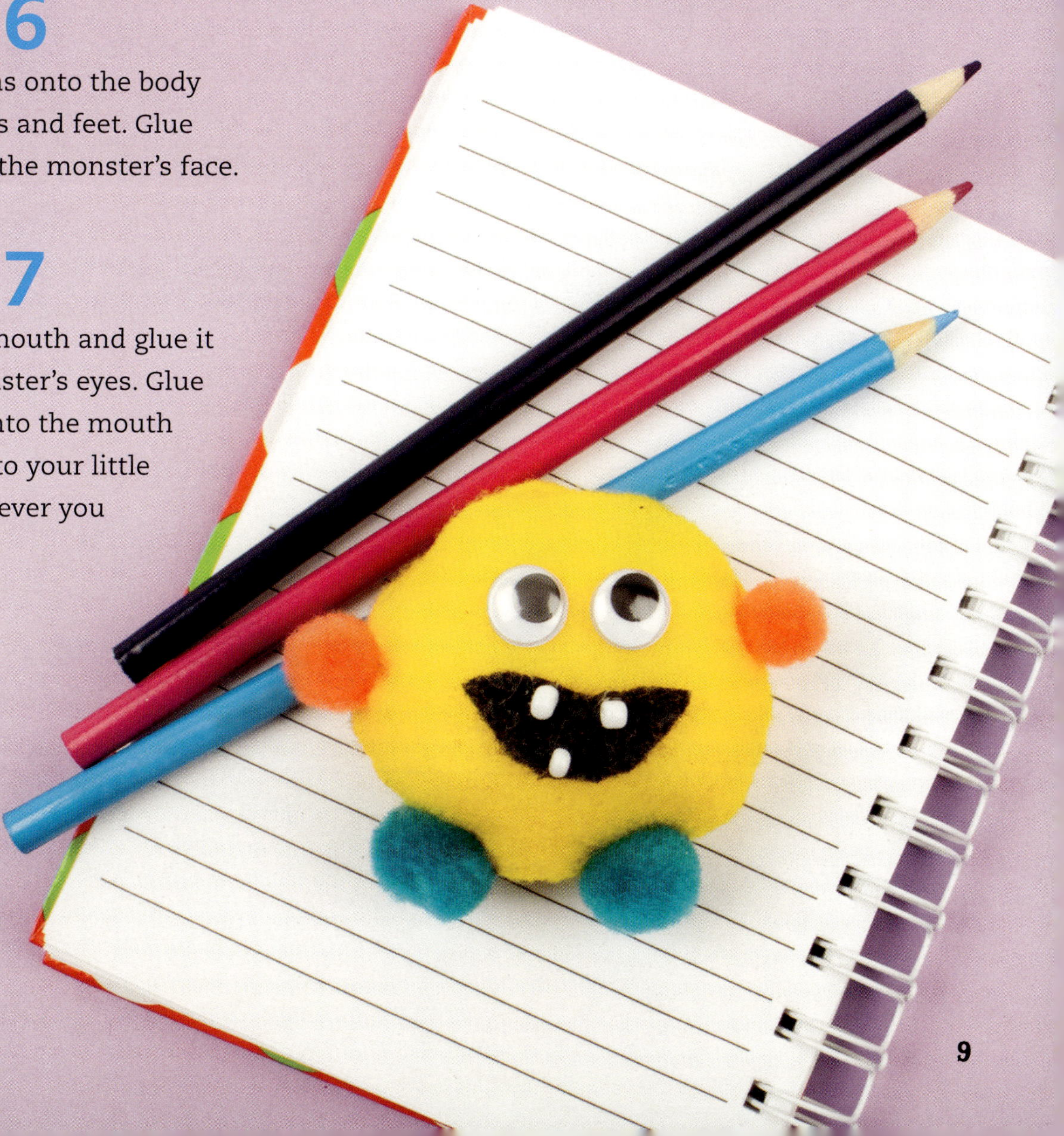

# Mini BULLETIN BOARD

Post tiny pictures and messages on this teeny-weeny bulletin board!

**MATERIALS**

- » cork tile
- » ruler
- » craft knife
- » wooden stir sticks
- » scissors
- » hot-glue gun
- » push pins, paper, stickers and more for decorating

### 1

Use a craft knife to cut a 7.5 × 5-cm rectangle out of cork.

### 2

Cut a 7.5-cm piece of wooden stir stick. Cut the ends at an angle to create a trapezoid. Repeat to cut another stir stick.

### 3

Glue the stir stick pieces on the long sides of the cork rectangle. The longer edge of each piece should face out.

### 4

Cut two 5-cm pieces from a wooden stir stick. Again, cut the ends at an angle.

## 5

Glue the 5-cm pieces along the short sides of the cork rectangle. Their angled ends should line up with the angled ends of the longer pieces.

## 6

Cut two more 7.5-cm pieces and two more 5-cm pieces from the stir sticks. Do not cut the ends at angles. Glue the four pieces along the outside edges of the cork rectangle to complete your mini bulletin board.

## 7

Decorate your bulletin board with little stickers, messages and drawings!

# Mini ZEN GARDEN

**MATERIALS**
- » large jar lid
- » fine sand
- » pebbles
- » thin wooden skewer
- » ruler
- » scissors
- » hot-glue gun

Rake designs into your mini Zen garden any time you need a moment of mindfulness!

## 1

Fill the lid with fine sand. Place a few pebbles in the sand.

## 2

Cut a 5-cm piece and a 2.5-cm piece of a thin wooden skewer. Glue the middle of the small piece to one end of the long piece to make a T shape. This is the rake for your garden.

## 3

Cut three 1.3-cm pieces from the wooden skewer. Glue them to the end of the rake so they stick out like tines.

## 4

Use the rake to make ripples and waves in the sand!

### TINY TIP
Add tiny plants or trinkets to your Zen garden to make it your own!

# Mini DRAWER FRESHENERS

Keep sock drawers, wardrobes and other small spaces smelling fresh with these mini scented rice sachets!

**MATERIALS**
- » white rice
- » measuring cups and spoons
- » paper cup
- » craft stick
- » essential oil
- » 12-cm lid (roughly)
- » pencil
- » cotton fabric
- » scissors
- » string

## 1

Pour 60 grams of white rice into a paper cup. Use a craft stick to stir 8 to 10 drops of essential oil into the rice.

## 2

Use the lid to trace a circle onto a piece of cotton fabric.

## 3

Cut out the fabric circle and lay it flat on your work surface. If there is a pattern on one side of the fabric, the pattern side should be facing downwards.

**4**

Scoop 15 grams of the rice mixture into the centre of the fabric circle.

**5**

Cut a 20-cm length of string. Gather the fabric around the rice and tie the string around the gathered fabric. Knot the string twice to secure.

**6**

Repeat steps 2 to 5 to make more mini drawer fresheners. Add them to any space that needs a refresh!

# Mini TERRARIUM

**This tiny ecosystem waters itself through the cycle of evaporation and condensation.**

## MATERIALS

- » clean, empty spice jar with lid
- » paper
- » soil
- » tweezers
- » moss
- » pebbles
- » small plant, such as fern or ivy
- » trinket or small toy (optional)
- » water dropper

### 1
Use a piece of paper to funnel soil into the jar. The jar should be about one-third full of soil.

### 2
Use tweezers to place a few small pieces of moss on top of the soil.

### 3
Place several pebbles on top of the moss.

### 4
Use tweezers to plant a few bits of a small plant in the soil. Add a trinket or small toy for decoration if you like.

## 5

Water your tiny terrarium with a few drops from a water dropper.

## 6

Screw on the lid and place the jar near a window. The lid will keep the soil and plants from drying out, meaning you do not have to water them! If you choose to leave the lid off, use the water dropper to keep the soil damp.

# Mini LAMP

**This cosy mini lamp is the perfect tiny night light!**

## MATERIALS

- » cork
- » paint and paintbrush
- » push pin
- » 30 cm of thin wire
- » LED tea light
- » patterned paper
- » ruler
- » scissors
- » hot-glue gun
- » string
- » gems

## 1

Paint the cork a colour of your choice and let it dry.

## 2

Stick a push pin into one end of the cork.

## 3

Wrap the wire a few times around the push pin. Then wrap it around the bulb of the LED tea light. Continue wrapping the wire around the bulb to securely attach it to the push pin.

## 4

Cut a strip of patterned paper that is ½ cm taller than the tea light and long enough to wrap around it. Glue the paper around the tea light, leaving the extra ½ cm hanging off the bulb end like a lampshade.

## 5

Cut a 2.5-cm piece of string. Glue gems along the string, leaving the last ½ cm uncovered. Glue the uncovered string end to the inside of the lampshade so the gems hang down from it.

## 6

Repeat step 5 to add gem strings around the entire lampshade. If you'd like, vary the string sizes so the gems hang at different lengths.

## 7

Put the mini lamp up on its cork base. Turn on the LED to make it glow!

# Mini FRAME MAGNETS

**MATERIALS**

- » craft sticks
- » scissors
- » ruler
- » hot-glue gun
- » air-dry clay
- » toothpick
- » paint and paintbrush
- » patterned paper or small photo
- » magnet

**Sculpt your own mini frames to hang on a fridge or freezer!**

### 1

Cut two pieces of craft stick that are 2.5 cm long and two pieces that are 5 cm long.

### 2

Glue the four pieces together to form a rectangular frame.

## 3

Place a strip of air-dry clay over each side of the frame.

## 4

Use your fingers to mould the clay around the frame so the craft sticks no longer show.

**TINY TIP**
Use extra bits of clay to add 3D designs to your frame!

## 5

Use a toothpick to add texture to the clay. Let the clay dry. It will take about a day to dry.

## 6

Once the clay is dry, paint the frame.

## 7

Cut a 5 × 2.5-cm photo or piece of patterned paper.

## 8

Glue the paper or photo to the back of your frame. The back of the paper or photo should face upwards.

## 9

Glue a magnet to the back of the paper or photo. Then hang your mini frame magnet!

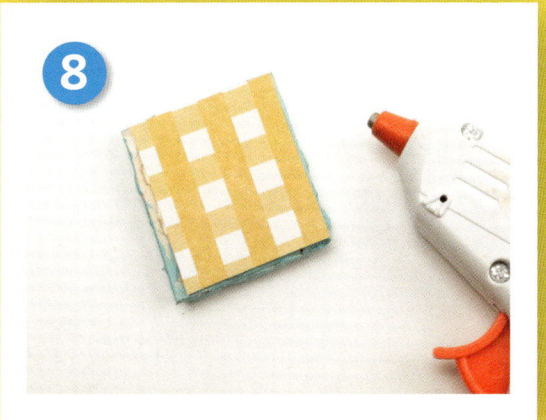

# Mini BAG THROW

Keep this mini bag throw game handy for when you need a quick homework break!

## MATERIALS

- » empty rectangular tissue box
- » ruler
- » marker pen
- » craft knife
- » circular lid
- » duct tape or paint and paintbrushes
- » scrap fabric in 2 colours
- » scissors
- » hot-glue gun
- » rice
- » measuring spoons

## 1

Turn the empty tissue box over so the bottom is facing up. Use a ruler and marker pen to draw a line from the top left to the bottom right on one long side of the box.

## 2

On the other long side of the box, draw a line from the top right to the bottom left.

## 3

Use a craft knife to cut along the lines you made. Then cut along a top and bottom edge of the box's short sides to separate the two halves of the box.

# 4

Recycle the half of the box with the tissue opening. Place the other half on your work surface so the bottom of the box is facing up. Trace a lid to make a circle near the top end of the wedge.

# 5

Use the craft knife to cut out the circle. This is your throwing board.

25

## 6

Use duct tape or paint to decorate the throwing board.

## 7

Cut eight squares with 5-cm sides from a piece of scrap fabric. Cut eight more squares of the same size from another colour of scrap fabric.

## 8

Pair up the squares so you have four pairs of each colour of fabric. For each pair, place one square on top of the other so the patterned sides are facing in. Glue the squares together along three edges, leaving the fourth edge unglued.

## 9

Turn the glued square pouches inside out so the patterned side of the fabric is now facing out.

# 10

Fill each pouch with roughly 7.5 to 15 ml rice. Then fold the open edges inwards and glue them together with the hot-glue gun to create a clean seam. Now your bags are ready to throw!

# Mini TAPESTRY

**Make a cute cardboard loom for weaving a charming mini tapestry!**

## MATERIALS
- » cardboard
- » ruler
- » scissors
- » marker pen
- » wool in several colours
- » tape
- » hair grip

## 1
Cut a rectangle of cardboard that is 10 cm long and 5.7 cm wide.

## 2
Make a mark every ½ cm along the short sides of the rectangle. Cut a 1.5-cm slit into the cardboard at each mark. This creates a loom frame.

## 3
Thread a piece of wool into the top-left slit. Leave a 5-cm tail of wool on the back side of the cardboard. Tape it down.

## 4

Pull the wool down the front side of the cardboard and into the first slit on the bottom left of the loom.

## 5

Wrap the wool around the back of the cardboard and bring it back up through the next slit on the top.

## 6

Continue this pattern until you have eight vertical lengths of wool across your loom. Leave another 5-cm tail and tape it down on the back side of the loom.

## 7

Cut a small rectangular strip of cardboard and slip it between the wool strands and the loom. This keeps the wool lifted so you can weave under it.

## 8

Cut two 10-cm pieces of wool to start your fringe layer. Fold the strands in half and thread them behind the two vertical strands on the far right. Pull the free ends of the strands through the folded loop and pull to tighten the knot.

## 9

Repeat step 8 with the remaining pairs of vertical strands, using a different colour wool for each pair.

## 10

Cut 30 cm of your first wool colour. Loop the wool through a hair grip. Weave the hair grip under the first vertical strand on the bottom right side of the loom, then over the next. Keep weaving the grip through the strands, alternating between over and under.

## 11

When you reach the other side, pull the wool through the vertical strands, leaving a 2.5-cm tail on the right side.

## 12

Weave the hair grip back from left to right, reversing the pattern from step 10. So, you will weave over the first string, under the next one, and so on.

## 13

Continue weaving until you have a 2.5-cm tail of wool. When you want to switch to a new colour of wool, knot the two loose ends of wool and cut off any excess.

## 14

Repeat steps 10 to 13 with each wool colour. Stop weaving about 2.5 cm from the top of the loom.

## 15

When you've finished weaving, remove the bottom loops of wool from the loom. Unstick the tails from the back side of the loom and carefully remove the top loops from the loom.

## 16

Knot the left tail and the first loop together. Then knot the first loop and the second loop together. Continue until you have knotted the correct tail with the last loop.

## 17

Tie the ends of the two tails together to create a hanger for your tapestry!

# FIND OUT MORE

## BOOKS

*10-Minute Crafty Projects* (10-Minute Makers), Elsie Olson (Raintree, 2022)

*Sand Art* (Awesome Art), Jeanette Ryall (Raintree, 2021)

*Spring Crafts From Different Cultures* (Multicultural Seasonal Crafts), Megan Borgert-Spaniol (Raintree, 2023)

## WEBSITES

**www.bbc.co.uk/cbeebies/makes/lets-go-club-ten-minute-crafts?collection=the-lets-go-club-craft-activities**
The CBeebies website has lots of quick craft activities to do.

**www.goodhousekeeping.com/home/craft-ideas/g39762537/crafts-for-kids/**
Find ideas for some easy craft activities on this website.

## ABOUT THE AUTHOR

**Megan Borgert-Spaniol** is an author and editor of children's media. When she isn't writing or reading, she enjoys doing yoga, eating croissants and making homemade pizzas. Megan lives in Minneapolis, USA, with a tall, goofy man and a small, chatty cat.